THE BREAD OF LIFE

The Bread of Life

*Scripture Readings and Reflections
to Prepare for the Eucharist*

David E. Rosage

Servant Books
Ann Arbor, Michigan

ISBN 0-89283-067-0

Dedicated

To all those who have made my priestly ministry a happy, joyous, peaceful experience and to all my brother priests who daily offer the Eucharist in our name as a gift to the Father in union with Jesus sanctified by the Holy Spirit.

Contents

INTRODUCTION

W E are a eucharistic people who have the unique privilege of offering the Eucharist frequently, even daily. In our lifetime, we may celebrate the Eucharist thousands of times. Being human, we have a natural tendency to take so much for granted. How easily we can lack or even lose a deep appreciation for the Eucharist—its purpose, its real significance.

Often we need to ask ourselves some probing questions. Why is it that despite hundreds of thousands of Masses daily and weekly, Christians continue to live ordinary, mundane lives? Can we really distinguish Mass-going Christians from other Christians? How many Catholics go to Mass as an act of private devotion with little or no awareness of the truth that the Eucharist is essentially a corporate action of the whole community? Have we lost the awareness that we are incorporated into the entire body of Christ? How many of us go to Mass to receive Jesus in Holy Communion and thereby gain an increase of grace or to pile up a few "brownie points" for ourselves?

These are some hard questions which go to the very root of our daily life and practice. They are poignant questions, but we need to pause, to reflect and to listen from time to time to assess our own appreciation of, and our own attitude toward, the Eucharist.

Not Of The World

The eucharistic celebration, like many other aspects of our Christian way of life, has been influenced and often subordinated to the pressures of our society. Many of the attitudes of our present-day culture, be they humanism, materialism, sexism, have tended to make the Eucharist conform to their values. We have retained the words of the Eucharist, but often lost their meaning and real significance. For many of us the Mass is not yet the sacrament of unity.

St. Paul severely criticized the Christians at Corinth, whom he loved dearly, for their lack of appreciation of the Eucharist. He said that the Eucharist which they were offering was valid, but not very fruitful because of their lack of charity. He thundered: "When you assemble, it is not to eat the Lord's Supper, for everyone is in haste to eat his own supper. One person goes hungry, while another gets drunk..." (1 Cor 11:20). The transformation into the image of Jesus was not taking place in their lives because of their lack of love of neighbor. Instead St. Paul said: "That is why many among you are sick and infirm, and why so many are dying" (1 Cor 11:30).

In the Constitution on the Sacred Liturgy, the Second Vatican Council reiterates Paul's admonition when it teaches: "In order that the Liturgy may be able to produce its full effects, it is necessary that the faithful come to it with proper dispositions, that their minds should be attuned to their voices, and that they should cooperate with divine grace lest they receive it in vain" (Par. 11).

Some Christians have the attitude that the Eucharist possesses almost magical powers of transformation. This attitude implies that if Mass is celebrated, the fruits of the sacrifice and the sacrament are automatically operative within us. This is true to some extent, but we cannot afford to neglect prayerful preparation and reflection, awareness, and attitudes that would permit the sacraments to be fruitful in our lives.

The liturgy must be related to our lives. It is a celebration of all that we are and do. It is easy to make the liturgy a thing apart, to relegate it to the realm of the sacred, being far less demanding of us that way.

Yet, the Council speaks to us when it sets forth this directive: "The Church, therefore, earnestly desires that Christ's faithful....should be instructed by God's word and nourished at the table of the Lord's body; they should give thanks to God; by offering the Immaculate Victim, not only through the hands of the priest, but also with him, they should learn to offer themselves; through Christ the Mediator, they should be drawn day by day into ever more perfect union with God and with each other, so that finally God may be all in all." (Constitution on the Sacred Liturgy par. 48).

Study

In our private lives we can come to a deeper appreciation of the Eucharist by spending time in study. Modern biblical scholarship has opened for us many new and exciting avenues to a richer, fuller understanding of the Eucharist. This furnishes us

with a wealth of material for our own study and reflection. One consequence of our study will be an
emphasis not so much on the number of Masses we
offer, but rather on the depth of commitment we
are willing to make because of our better understanding of the Mass. Then we will see more clearly
that the Eucharist is a life-style to be lived daily;
that the Eucharist is not a reality apart from our
daily routine so often immersed in the temporalities
of daily survival.

Prayer

As we spend time in prayer contemplating the
Eucharist, we shall come to appreciate more fully
the richness and the depth of the Mass in our lives.
It is the mystery of faith, into which our prayer will
give us a deeper insight. The time spent in contemplative prayer will draw us into a more personal
relationship with Jesus, our eternal Highpriest. As
we get to know him better with our hearts, our love
for him will grow and our understanding of the
total gift he made of himself will increase.

Our response in love will be the greater. We will
desire to give ourselves as graciously and as generously as Jesus gave himself. As our love for him
matures we will want to be identified with Jesus, to
be one with him. This will be the fruit of our
prayer.

Transformation

As we celebrate the Eucharist, it will challenge
our life-style. For many, the Mass and all it stands
for is only a veneer covering a rather secular way of

life. We even implore Jesus to sanction and bless our views and endeavors which may be completely at odds with his gospel. For some Christians there is nothing which would set them apart from anyone else in society.

Jesus did not come into the world to reinforce the world in its secular life-style by the consolation of his presence. He came to transform and save the world. At Mass Jesus transforms us in two ways. First, as we expose our thinking to God's word as it is read and explained to us in the Liturgy of the Word, a conversion begins to take place within us even though we may not be consciously aware of it. Jesus could say of the transforming power of his Word: "You are clean already, thanks to the word I have spoken to you" (Jn 15:3). The author of Hebrews describes the power of his Word in this way: "God's word is living and effective, sharper than any two-edged sword" (Heb 4:12).

The second way in which Jesus transforms us is by inviting us to join him in making a complete gift of ourselves to the Father. The Second Vatican Council reminds Christians that "they should learn to offer themselves; through Christ the Mediator, they should be drawn day by day into ever perfect union with God and with each other, so that God may be all in all" (Constitution of The Sacred Liturgy par. 48).

When we contemplate the loving offering Jesus made of himself, we will want to unite ourselves more generously with him. This will draw us into an ever more perfect union with God and with each other.

Commitment

Jesus calls us to follow him. He then conditions us as he prepares us to follow more closely in his footsteps. After this Jesus asks us to commit ourselves to our vocation. As we celebrate the Eucharist with Jesus, we should be led to commit ourselves more generously to him.

We can hardly say our "Amen" without at the same time accepting his command to love one another as he loved us. Jesus said imperatively: "Do this in remembrance of me." This is not merely a command to perform an outward ceremony, but an injunction to do what Jesus did: to commit ourselves as totally as he did. His life of service was unto death.

If we come to share at the table of the Lord without adopting his values and without committing ourselves to putting them into practice in our daily living, then we separate what we do from the totality of the self-gift which it represented for Jesus. For him it was a genuine kenosis. Otherwise, we expect to receive from the Lord without responding in love.

This gift of self depends upon our response in love. To be a disciple of Jesus is to love so completely that we cannot help but be totally his. Jesus loves us so infinitely that he could give nothing less than the total gift of himself, the very last drop of his blood. He says: "As the Father has loved me so I have loved you" (Jn 15:9). In the Eucharist he is awaiting our response. Can our response be anything less?

How to Use This Book

The themes which are suggested for each day of the month are a sort of launching pad into prayer. Read the whole scripture selection reflectively, permitting every word to find a home in your heart. Pause and rest with a word or an expression which speaks to you.

The brief reflections which are presented are offered only as a possible suggestion for prayer, a pathway leading into prayer, or as a stimulus to focus your attention on some phase of the Eucharist. By all means let the Holy Spirit guide you into prayer.

As we prayerfully approach the Mass each day, we will discover the truth of the words of the Constitution on the Sacred Liturgy: "From the liturgy, therefore, and especially from the Eucharist, as from a font, grace is poured forth upon us; and the sanctification of men in Christ and the glorification of God, to which all other activities of the Church are directed as toward their end, is achieved in the most efficacious possible way" (Par. 10).

Inspired by the Holy Spirit, St. Paul states the same truth in different words. He tells us: "All of us, gazing on the Lord's glory with unveiled faces, are being transformed from glory to glory into his very image by the Lord who is Spirit" (2 Cor 3:18).

At Eucharist we pray:"Let your Spirit come upon these gifts to make them holy, so that they may become for us the body and blood of our Lord, Jesus Christ." With the guidance of that same Holy Spirit, may the thoughts which are presented in these pages make us more receptive to the powerful operation of the Holy Spirit within us: "so that they may become *for us* the body and blood of our Lord, Jesus Christ."

ONE

MANNA AND THE EUCHARIST

Exodus 16:4-15

ONE must spend some time in a desert like Sinai, surrounded by the barrenness of rocks and sand, in order to appreciate more fully God's loving and providential care of his Chosen People. In the desert there was no source of food or drink. Humanly speaking, survival was impossible. The Israelites had to depend totally on God's providential love. God did not abandon them. He fed them miraculously with manna and quail. Likewise by his divine power he supplied them with water when there was no natural source of water.

The history of God's providential care and the miraculous means he used to supply all the needs of his people were an ideal preparation for the gift of the Holy Eucharist to come centuries later. Just as the Israelites had to have faith and trust in God, so Jesus asked for faith in himself when he was about to give us the gift of himself hidden under the species of bread and wine.

Like the Israelites, we are wandering through the desert of life in this land of exile. We are on our pilgrimage to the Promised Land—our union with our loving Father for all eternity.

In the desert of Sinai, God's caring love supplied the only means of survival for the Chosen People; likewise, through the Holy Eucharist, Jesus has supplied us with all our needs for our journey. Like the Israelites, we need food for our journey. Each day Jesus invites us to the inexhaustible fount of nourishment in the eucharistic banquet.

Each day as we come to join our eternal Highpriest in celebrating the Eucharist, we are assured that we are not journeying alone, but that Jesus is with us and within us every step of the way. As the lyrics of one modern song proclaims: "Lord Jesus, you shall be our song as we journey . . ."

The Mass is the very source in which we find hope and encouragement when the road seems rough and the traveling quite difficult if not seemingly impossible. Our courage and strength are renewed as we meet Jesus in his eucharistic celebration.

When life's deserts are hot, the mountains high and the valleys deep, we find great comfort and joy in the awareness that Jesus loves us. His presence in the Eucharist speaks to our heart of his overwhelming love, a love which wants to be with us at all times.

When we contemplate God's loving presence among us, our hearts can certainly exclaim with the Israelites: "Manna — what is this?"

To continue your contemplation on this theme we suggest:

John 6:25-31 — Look beyond perishable food
Psalm 78:1-72 — Manna rained from heaven

TWO

GOD'S INVITATION

Isaiah 55:1-13

Our gracious Father invites us to the banquet he has prepared for us. How aptly this invitation can be adapted to the eucharistic banquet and how effectively it can prepare us for the Eucharist.

"All you who are thirsty." Our hearts are always "thirsty," seeking something beyond ourselves. Whether we are aware of it or not, our hearts are always seeking a more personal relationship with God. We find that closer relationship with Jesus in each Mass.

"Come to the water." Water is the source of life. In scriptural language "living water" always means divine life. The Eucharist is the very source of divine life.

"Let the scoundrel forsake his way----" In the penitential rite of the Mass we recognize that our ways are often not God's ways. We are invited to examine our thoughts and ask for healing and forgiveness.

"Come, without paying and without cost----" In the Mass we bring the gift of ourselves. At best our

gift is often half-hearted and self-centered. Jesus adds the gift of himself to our gift. In fact, at the consecration he changes our gifts of bread and wine into his own body and blood. Thus he gives himself to the Father in our name.

"So shall my word be that goes forth from my mouth——" In the Liturgy of the Word, Jesus himself speaks to us. There is power in his Word to mold and transform our hearts if we but listen. The Father, too, invites us to listen.

"Yes, in joy you shall depart." At the time of dismissal at Mass we are reminded that Jesus has become Eucharist for us. Now we should go forth as witnesses and become Eucharist to others.

"In peace you shall be brought back." As we go forth to reflect the love of Jesus to others, as we permit him to love others through us, we shall return to the Eucharist in peace — that peace which the world cannot give.

In your contemplative prayer, listen to Jesus' invitation:

Luke 14:16-24 — Jesus invites you

Hosea 6:1-3 — God always invites us back

THREE

JESUS PREPARES THE WAY

John 6:1-15

JESUS was always sensitive to all the needs of his followers. At times Jesus was asked to heal only physical affliction, but he went beyond and healed the whole person. He healed physically, spiritually, and psychologically.

When Jesus multiplied the loaves and fishes, he not only supplied the present need for food, but his loving concern and power gave promise and reassurance that he would continue to provide for all our needs even today. These needs are amply provided through the Eucharist.

First, Jesus manifested his loving concern for those pilgrims when he asked: "Where shall we get bread for these people to eat?" John tells us: "He knew well what he intended to do."

In the Eucharist, Jesus manifests this same loving concern for each one of us. He loves us and wants to be with us always. He recognizes our need for him and he graciously supplies that need.

Secondly, before Jesus took action to relieve their

needs, he wanted the apostles to recognize their own helplessness, their own inability to feed this vast crowd. This poverty of spirit is essential before God can act in us.

The same is true today. Jesus wants us to acknowledge our own poverty of spirit. "Apart from me, you can do nothing." When we humbly admit our inability, then Jesus proceeds to supply all our needs by his very presence and power in the Eucharist.

Thirdly, Jesus asks for faith in him. In spite of the fact that the crowd was tired, restless, hungry, and eager to move along, Jesus gave the order: "Get the people to recline." This required great faith, because as soon as they sat down they rendered themselves helpless to care for their own needs. St. Mark adds his own personal touch when he says: "The people took their places in hundreds and fifties, neatly arranged like flower beds." When they manifested this deep faith in Jesus, they must have looked to him like beautiful flower beds.

Jesus asks for our faith in his hidden, but dynamic eucharistic presence. When we step out with a vibrant, operative faith, then Jesus responds most generously.

Fourthly, Jesus then fed them miraculously since there was more food left over than they had to start with.

In the Eucharist, Jesus supplies all our needs by the gift of himself. Nothing else really matters. "How deep are the riches and the wisdom and the knowledge of God!" (Rom 11:33).

To thank God for his goodness and greatness,
pray:
> Psalm 145 — The psalmist invites us to recall
>   the greatness and goodness of
>   God.
> Psalm 138 — The hymn of a grateful heart

FOUR

FOOD THAT REMAINS UNTO LIFE ETERNAL

John 6:52-58

As we swiftly and comfortably glide along superhighways, all our physical needs are conveniently supplied at almost every off-ramp. The beckoning signs, raised high above the road, invite us to refuel our vehicle, to rest comfortably, to replenish our strength by satisfying our hunger and thirst. All these conveniences make our journeying not only possible but pleasant and comfortable.

Our journey through life is a pilgrimage back to our loving Father. Each day we travel a part of that way. As we travel down the highway of life, we have many needs; we especially need food for the journey.

Jesus has given us himself in the Eucharist as our spiritual food to nourish us, to strengthen us, thus enabling us to continue life's journey. In fact, Jesus is quite emphatic in telling us that we will not complete our journey without him: "Let me solemnly assure you, if you do not eat the flesh of the Son of Man and drink his blood, you have no life in you"

(Jn 6:53). There is no alternative. Jesus is quite emphatic.

Unlike the venal hospitality in our society, Jesus supplies all our needs because he loves us. "Come to me, all you who are weary and find life burdensome, and I will refresh you" (Mt 11:28). He loves us so much, he is not content merely to supply our needs but he wants to be a part of our lives.

Napoleon used to say that he did not receive Holy Communion because he was not worthy to do so. Learned theologians tried to convince him otherwise without success. One day Napoleon engaged an old country pastor in the same discussion. The old pastor replied: "Sire, you are not worthy, but you need it." No one can ever be worthy. Jesus does not take into consideration our worthiness but our need.

Jesus is always present with us and within us, but he wants to give us this visible sign of his presence to reassure us of his presence and to strengthen our weak faith. He chose common, but symbolic signs: bread and wine, food and drink, thus accommodating himself to humanness.

Daily he invites us to come to his table: "All you who are thirsty, come to the water! You who have no money, come receive grain and eat; come, without paying and without cost" (Is 55:1).

Contemplate God's providential love in these passages:
　　Exodus 16:4-15 — Quail and manna from heaven
　　Matthew 6:25-34 — His eye is on the sparrow

FIVE

THE MASS: THE PERFECT ACT OF PRAISE

Matthew 22:15-21

ONE day the enemies of Jesus tried to trap him in his teachings. They asked him: "Is it lawful to pay tax to the emperor or not?" Whatever Jesus would answer, they felt certain that they had him trapped. However, Jesus took the occasion to teach a valuable lesson: "Give to Caesar what is Caesar's, but give to God what is God's."

Our first and prime duty to God is to offer him our praise. Praise is a perfect prayer because God alone is the object of our prayer. Even when we thank God, we are including ourselves in the prayer; by contrast, the prayer of praise is directed solely to God. God wants our praise. Listen to what he says to us through the psalmist:

"Offer to God praise as your sacrifice" (Ps 50:14).

"He that offers praise as a sacrifice glorifies me" (Ps 50:23).

The Eucharist is a perfect act of praise. We are not offering it alone. The entire Church throughout the world, the whole Body of Christ, joins us in offering each eucharistic celebration.

I met a man on a plane one time who was very much depressed about the standard of morality in the world and the difficulty of trying to rear children in this spiritually polluted atmosphere. He was not a Catholic and did not understand the Mass. However, as we streaked across the sky at some 30,000 feet, we could see the earth very clearly, even though there was a thin, cloudlike vapor rising from the earth upward. This gorgeous view gave me an idea.

I explained to him that the Mass was a perfect act of praise of God and that every two seconds there was another Mass beginning somewhere over the earth. This paean of praise rising from the earth like the vapor-cloud below us and ascending to God was not in vain and would counteract the myriad crimes disturbing the face of the earth. As Paul assures us: "Despite the increase of sin, grace has far surpassed it." Again Paul encourages us: "Do not be conquered by evil, but conquer evil with good" (Rom 12:21).

In the Eucharist we are united with Jesus our eternal Highpriest in offering our praise to God. Jesus adds an infinite dimension to our prayer of praise.

Already on earth Jesus offered praise to his Father: "Father, Lord of heaven and earth, to you I offer praise; for what you have hidden from the learned and the clever you have revealed to the merest children . . ." (Mt 11:25).

For additional prayer:
Matthew 6:19-24 — True riches
Psalm 148:1-14 — Hymn of all creation to the Almighty Creator

EUCHARISTIC PRAISE

John 17:1-5

As we contemplate the immensity of the heavens, the massive beauty of the mountains, the exquisite tint of the flowers, the melodious song of the birds, the gift of life, the warmth of being loved, our thoughts naturally turn to the Creator, the Lord and Master of the entire universe. Our hearts leap with joy because he is our Abba, our loving Father who knows every hair on our heads.

We want to sing his praises, to glorify his name, to adore him in his transcendence, to worship him in his almighty power. This is the rationale of the eucharistic celebration. It is a perfect sacrifice of praise made to the Father, offered by the Son, and sanctified by the Holy Spirit.

As Jesus was beginning to offer the first Mass at the Last Supper, he explained that this is a sacrifice of praise. "Now is the Son of Man glorified and God is glorified in him" (Jn 13:31).

In his highpriestly prayer, Jesus asked that his passion and death, which is represented in the Mass, might bring glory to the Father as well as to himself. Jesus prayed: "Father, the hour has come!

SIX

Give glory to your Son that your Son may give glory to you" (Jn 17:1).

The Mass is a magnificent prayer of praise to the Father, Son, and Holy Spirit. In the eucharistic celebration we respond jubilantly to the invitation of Jesus as we express our praise to the Holy Trinity.

In the Gloria we sing: "Glory to God in the highest . . . we worship you, we give you thanks, we praise you for your glory."

Then we turn to Jesus with these words: "For you alone are the Holy one, you alone are the Lord, you alone are the Most High, Jesus Christ, with the Holy Spirit in the glory of God the Father."

The purpose of the Mass is to praise God; hence, the prayers of the Mass are punctuated with words of praise and glory to the Trinity. The responsorial psalm is frequently a hymn of praise to the Father. In the words of one responsorial psalm, let us sing: "Praise the Lord from the earth . . . ."

To continue your contemplative prayer with the theme of praise, we suggest:
    Psalm 150 — A doxology
    Ephesians 1:3-10 — God calls us to praise him

SEVEN

EUCHARIST MEANS THANKSGIVING

Luke 17:11-19

WE all know from personal experience how painful ingratitude can be. Even Jesus felt keenly the ingratitude of the nine lepers. When only one of the ten who were cured returned to him, Jesus took the occasion to say: "Were not all ten made whole? Where are the other nine? Was there no one to return and give thanks to God except this foreigner?"

Jesus was always grateful to his Father. Repeatedly he thanked his Father for everything. When Jesus instituted the Holy Eucharist, he "gave thanks."

"Eucharist" means thanksgiving and gratitude. In the Mass we give back to the Father the gifts he has given us, the most precious of which is Jesus himself.

We express our love for another person by giving gifts. The greatest of all gifts is the gift of ourselves. The Eucharist is our most powerful means of giving. We unite ourselves to the gift of Jesus as he gives himself in our name to the Father.

The Eucharist is the solemn giving back to God the gifts he has so lavishly bestowed on us. At Mass we offer him material gifts which are highly symbolic. Bread and wine represent our food and drink, the necessities of life. When we offer what is essential for our existence, then we are giving the gift of self.

This offering is followed by the consecration when Jesus gives himself to the Father. This is his prayer to the Father. He has already united our thanks, the gift of ourselves, to his gift, to present to the Father.

Later on we have the opportunity to present the gift of ourselves to the Father in these words: "Through him, with him, in him, in the unity of the Holy Spirit, all glory and honor is yours almighty Father forever and ever." Our "Amen" makes the gift complete. Our "Amen" at the end of the Eucharistic Prayer is the gift of ourselves to the Father joined with the oblation of Jesus. It consecrates us with him and in him. Amen! At one time, especially in the small churches at Rome, the "Amen" would resound like a clap of thunder through the edifice.

The psalmist asks himself: "How shall I make a return to the Lord for all the good he has done for me?" He answers his own question in these beautiful words: "The cup of salvation I will take up, and I will call upon the name of the Lord" (Ps 116:12).

How better can we express our prayer than in these words of the psalmist!

To continue your prayer of thanksgiving, read:
1 Thessalonians 5:16-18 — Render constant
thanks
1   Chronicles   16:8-36 — Give   thanks   to   the
Lord for he is good

EIGHT

THE MASS:
A PRAYER OF INTERCESSION

John 14:12-14

ONE of the most touching examples of intercession on a human level is the biblical account of
Jonathan interceding with his father, Saul, on
David's behalf (1 Sm 19:1-7). Jonathan was mo-
tivated to intercede for David because he dearly
loved his friend David. Likewise, Jesus remains our
intercessor because of his infinite love for each one
of us.

The Mass is the most perfect prayer of intercession because Jesus, the eternal highpriest and prin-
cipal offerer of the Mass, is the perfect intercessor
between God and man since he is the God-man.
"God is one. One also is the mediator between God
and man, the man Jesus Christ who gave himself as
a ransom for all" (1 Tm 2:5).

Jesus is our intercessor before the Father. At this
very moment, as the risen and glorified Lord, he is
at the right hand of the Father interceding for us.
Intercession is his ministry and his glorification. For
thirty years on earth Jesus lived a hidden life. For
three years he led a public life, preaching and doing

the works of the Father. Now for two thousand years he is interceding for us. As the inspired writer put it: "Jesus has a priesthood which does not pass away. Therefore he is always able to save those who approach God through him, since he forever lives to make intercession for them" (Heb 7:24-25).

Repeatedly Jesus encouraged us to ask in his name. "All you ask the Father in my name he will give you" (Jn 15:16). He himself will respond to our intercession: "Anything you ask me in my name I will do." (Jn 14:13). Jesus gave us hope when he said: "I give you my assurance whatever you ask the Father, he will give you in my name" (Jn 16:23).

Jesus not only encouraged us to intercede in his name, but he invites us to join him in the Eucharist, that he may join our prayer with his powerful intercession before the Father on our behalf. What hope and comfort! What a privilege and power is ours as we celebrate the Eucharist with Jesus in this land of exile!

Contemplate the powerful intercessory role of Jesus as found in:

1 John 2:1-2 — Jesus is our intercessor in
heaven

Romans 8:28-34 — Jesus is our mediator before
the Father

NINE

MARY, OUR INTERCESSOR AT MASS

John 2:1-11

CANA is a delightful story of loving concern.
Mary's maternal solicitude moved her to intercede with her Son even though his hour had not yet come. The loving heart of Jesus could not turn a deaf ear to his Mother's intercession.

Jesus used this occasion to reveal to us the power of his Mother's intercession; also, to teach us Mary's role as Mother of the Church and intercessor for her children. Changing water into wine is a symbolic sign and a remote preparation for the Eucharist.

At the very first Mass offered on Calvary's heights, Mary again fulfilled her role of intercessor. John gives us this brief account without adjective or adverb, yet so descriptive: "Near the cross of Jesus there stood his Mother" (Jn 19:25).

Mary's oblation was totally in union with that of her Son. She had said "Yes" to the Father just as her Son had done. Her heart, united with the heart of her Son, pleaded, "Father, forgive them...." The Father accepted the oblation of Jesus and his Mother.

35

Mary's role was climaxed on Calvary when Jesus gave us his Mother. What pathos, what tenderness, what depth of meaning in his words, "There is your Mother" (Jn 19:26).

The Church has always incorporated Mary's role in the Mass. Mary is the channel through which Jesus came to us. She is also the channel through which we go to Jesus.

In the forepart of the Mass we pray: "I ask blessed Mary, ever virgin...to pray for me to the Lord our God."

Then we continue in Eucharistic Prayer I: "In union with the whole Church we honor Mary, the ever-virgin Mother of Jesus Christ our Lord and God....May their merits and prayers gain us your constant help and protection." A similar petition is expressed in the other Eucharistic Prayers.

As we discover Mary's role as intercessor, we rediscover Jesus' gift to us of his Mother.

As Queen-Mother of our eternal Highpriest, Mary continues to intercede in heaven as she did on earth. Her intercession at Nazareth drew down our Redeemer. Her intercession on Calvary opened the flood gates of God's mercy. Her intercession in the Upper Room called down the Holy Spirit upon the disciples, and the Church was born.

Mary's role as intercessor began with her "Fiat" at the Annunciation and also at the Presentation in the Temple:

Luke 1: 26-38 — Mary's canticle
Luke 2:22-40 — Jesus in the temple

TEN

INTERCESSION OF THE ANGELS AND SAINTS

Revelation 5:11-14

In the tradition of the Church, we have always called upon the angels and saints and the whole heavenly court to intercede for us. We especially ask them to intercede for us at Mass. The author of Hebrews asks: "Are they not all ministering spirits, sent to serve those who are to inherit salvation?" (Heb 1:14).

The saints in heaven continue to intercede with Jesus even as they did on earth. They are our closest friends. They know and understand our needs. St. Paul assures us: "You are fellow citizens of the saints and members of the household of God" (Eph 2:19). The saints are also friends of Jesus and he does listen to their intercession.

In Eucharistic Prayer I we pray: "Almighty God we pray that your angel may take this sacrifice to your altar in heaven. . . ."

Again in Eucharistic Prayer II we plead: "Have mercy on us all! Make us worthy to share eternal life with Mary, the Virgin Mother of God, with the apostles and with all the saints who have done your will throughout the ages. May we praise you in union with them, and give you glory through your son, Jesus Christ."

In Eucharistic Prayer III we continue to intercede in communion with the saints: "May he make us an everlasting gift to you and enable us to share in the inheritance of your saints, with Mary the Virgin Mother of God; with the apostles, the martyrs and all your saints, on whose constant intercession we rely for help."

With Jesus the whole Church intercedes. This means we intercede with Mary, the Mother of the Church, with the angels, with the saints and with all our brothers and sisters here on earth. This is what intercession is all about — union with Jesus in what he is actually doing right now at the throne of the Father. The Church is most Church when it is assembled in union with Jesus, our eternal Highpriest, with all the angels and saints interceding for the coming of the kingdom. This is what the Eucharist is all about. May we give thanks to the Father for having made us worthy to share the lot of the saints in light. Read Ephesians 1:3-14.

Jesus invites us to intercede with him:
Matthew 9:35-38 — Intercessory prayer
Luke 22:39-46 — Power of prayer

ELEVEN

PREPARATION FOR MASS

Luke 22:7-13

Every host and hostess is well aware how much planning and preparation is necessary to entertain a number of guests at dinner. The dining room decor, the table arrangements, the little embellishments on the food all add to the enjoyment of the meal. The conviviality of the social hour preceding the dinner also adds to the enrichment of sharing a meal with those we love.

Jesus sent Peter and John into the city to prepare for the greatest meal on earth, the Last Supper, at which Jesus instituted the Holy Eucharist. The foreknowledge of Jesus of the person they were to meet and the place which was to be used added greatly to the mystery of that significant event. That Upper Room, or Cenacle, has become a hallowed spot because of what took place there. Every place where Mass is celebrated becomes a hallowed spot because of the eucharistic presence of Jesus there and the infinite love and power which radiates from the Mass.

It is impossible for our human minds to grasp the significance of the presence, the power and the fruits which accrue to us from the Mass. For this reason we need time to prepare for each celebration of the Eucharist.

We need some quiet time to lay aside the preoccupations of each day. We need to make some effort to eliminate all the busyness which clutters our hearts and minds. We need to refocus our attention on what we are about to do. We need time to orient ourselves Godward.

Jesus warned us that without proper preparation our reverence for him could become routine observance. He said of the Pharisees: "This people pays me lip service, but their heart is far from me" (Mt 15:8).

A complaint heard frequently is: "I don't get anything out of Mass." The response to that is quite obvious: How much do you put into it? Do you prayerfully prepare to offer each Mass?

In the Mass we are involved in a profound mystery. To be involved in that mystery we need orientation and prayerful preparation. We must contemplate the infinite love which motivates Jesus to continue his redemptive work in us through his eucharistic presence and power. We need to hear God speaking to us through the psalmist: "Be still and know that I am God" (Ps 46:11).

Some suggested scriptural passages to help us to prepare for the Eucharistic celebration:

Luke 3:1-6 — The prophet's advice
Luke 10:1-6 — Preparation for the coming of Jesus

TWELVE

OUR UNIQUE PRIVILEGE

Luke 22:14-20

DURING the course of a retreat for handicapped people, we celebrated the eucharistic liturgy out-of-doors under a canopy of majestic oak trees. The altar was surrounded by a halo of forty-four wheelchairs. As I observed the beaming faces encircling me, I was deeply touched. The exuberant joy radiating from the happy faces of these suffering people related its own story of how seldom most of them ever had the privilege of offering the Eucharist. How seldom they were able to enjoy the fresh air of the outdoors.

Their joy lifted my spirits and I rejoiced with them. I rejoiced once again in what it means to be a priest. What an awesome privilege to make Jesus eucharistically present for them. What an honor and joy to say to each one of them at communion time: "The body of Christ."

I could experience in some slight way how Jesus must have felt when he said: "I have greatly desired to eat this Passover with you before I suffer" (Lk 22:15).

A deep sense of gratitude filled my whole being as

I reflected on my privilege as a priest. I also felt a sense of regret for my own lack of appreciation for the Mass.

As a priest I can offer Mass at my own convenience at any hour of the day. Likewise, I can celebrate the Eucharist in such a variety of places, whereas these special friends of the Lord rarely have the opportunity even to go to Mass.

I could feel a richer realization of the unique privilege which is mine welling up within me. Hopefully with the grace of the eternal Highpriest, I will be able to celebrate the Eucharist with greater fervor.

I ask the Father to gift me, for Jesus said: "No one can come to me, unless the Father who sent me draws him" (Jn 6:44).

Jesus promised us that he would never leave us. "And know that I am with you always until the end of the world" (Mt 28:20). His eucharistic presence gives us visible tangible evidence that he has "made his dwelling among us" (Jn 1:14).

Like the apostles, we can meet Jesus on the shore of a lake, on the summit of a mountain, in the plain, in the desert, or in the crowded city. True to his promise, he is "with" us and "within" us. What a foretaste of heaven!

Continue praying with this theme using these suggested passages:

1 Corinthians 11:23-26 — The Lord's Supper
Acts 2:42-47 — The breaking of bread

THIRTEEN

EUCHARIST AS A MEAL

John 6:26-27

MUCH of our time and energy is taken up with food. Countless people are concerned with growing, producing, and preparing food. We entertain our friends by sharing our meal with them. We talk business over a meal. We eat to sustain our strength and energy, our very life itself.

In Sacred Scripture, a meal is symbolic and sacred. Jesus invites us to a sumptuous meal which has many dimensions. The Eucharist is a memorial, a sealing of a covenant, a thanksgiving, an expectation of the coming of the Lord, a presence, a prayer, a sacrifice of praise, a communion with Jesus and with one another. These are but a few of the dimensions of the Eucharist.

Jesus invites us to his banquet that our drooping spirits and our exhausted bodies may be replenished. His gentle invitation is like much music to our ears: "Come to me, all you who are weary and find life burdensome, and I will refresh you" (Mt 11:28).

Jesus not only invites us, but he makes our participation quite imperative if we are to live in union with him. When he instituted the Holy Eucharist he said: "Do this as a remembrance of me" (Lk 22:19).

Jesus wants us to come to the Eucharist not only for selfish motives, but because we love him and want to be united with him. Listen to his words to the men of his day and how aptly they can be addressed to us:

> "I assure you, you are not looking for me because you have seen signs, but because you have eaten your fill of the loaves. You should not be working for perishable food but for food that remains unto life eternal, food which the Son of Man will give you." (Jn 6:26-27)

Jesus wants us to come to the Eucharist:

- to open ourselves to receive the outpouring of his love.
- to unite ourselves with his highpriestly prayer of praise to the Father.
- to come together with our brothers and sisters to adore, worship, and thank our loving Father.
- to permit him to fill that longing and desire we have to be united with him.
- to remind us that he is dwelling within us in his risen glorified life.
- to nourish, sustain and strengthen us on our pilgrimage through life.

Some suggestions for continued contemplative prayer on this theme:

Matthew 22:1-10 — A unique invitation
Revelation 19:1-8 — Wedding banquet

FOURTEEN

THE MASS AND DISCIPLESHIP

Matthew 20:26-28

REPEATEDLY Jesus invites us to come and follow him. He calls us into discipleship. A disciple is more than a pupil. A disciple is one who absorbs the mentality and attitudes of the master so completely that he will not merely imitate the master, but will be identified with him.

Jesus invites us to follow him in offering the Eucharist. Jesus did not give us a ritual or formal cult to follow, but asked us to worship God with our whole mind, heart, and strength, and to love our neighbor as ourselves. If we believe in the Incarnation, then we must practice toward God the same kind of service that Jesus has shown us.

It is noteworthy that St. John devotes one fourth of his Gospel to the Last Supper, but never says a word about the consecration which we consider central to the Mass. Could it be that he wanted to show us that our whole life is brought to the Mass and that the whole eucharistic prayer is consecratory?

Notice that St. John does stress the entire role of Jesus at the Last Supper. He mentions the washing of the feet with Jesus' only vestment, a towel about his waist. At the Last Supper it was Jésus who cleansed the apostles, who provided the food, and nourished those who were present. He was in their midst as one who serves. "Such is the case with the Son of Man who has come, not to be served by others, but to serve, to give his own life as a ransom for the many" (Mt 20:28).

At the first Eucharist, Jesus reminds us of his own example: "I give you a new commandment. Love one another. Such as my love has been for you, so must your love be for each other. "This is how all will know you are my disciples: your love for one another" (Jn 13:34-35).

Jesus calls us into a life of service. For Jesus that first Mass was a total kenosis. If we are to be his disciples, then we too must strive to make our offering total and complete.

Unless we give ourselves as wholeheartedly as Jesus did in the first Eucharist, unless we translate our love into action for others, the words of the Eucharist are empty and devoid of real meaning and effect.

Ultimately, worship is not something we do and then offer it to God. Rather it is something we are. It is offering to God the image of Jesus come to perfection in us.

Reflect on these passages for further contemplation:
    John 12:24-26 – Total gift
    Luke 14:12-35 – Conditions for discipleship

FIFTEEN

THE GOOD SHEPHERD

John 10:1-18

How frequently and how appropriately the image of the shepherd appears in Scripture. In the Hebrew Testament, the Father says with paternal concern: "I myself will look after and tend my sheep" (Ez 34:11). In the Christian Testament, Jesus says with great tenderness: "I am the good shepherd" (Jn 10:11). This imagery spoke eloquently not only to the contemporaries of Jesus, but it also speaks poetically and prophetically to us today.

In the Eucharist, Jesus is both shepherd and lamb. He is the victim "Lamb that was slain." Jesus came to give his life for our redemption. He told us: "The Father loves me for this: that I lay down my life. . . . No one takes it from me: I lay it down freely" (Jn 10:17). The eucharistic celebration is a representation of Jesus' act of oblation and immolation.

In the Mass we also recall his role as shepherd. A shepherd loves and provides for his sheep. Jesus does that in each Mass. In his own words he assures us of this truth: "I came that they might have life and have it to the full" (Jn 10:10).

This imagery speaks to our hearts of the great love that Jesus has for each one of us. A shepherd loves and cares for his sheep. He gathers the scattered sheep when it is dark and cloudy. He leads them to nourishing pastures. He guards them while they lie down to rest.

Through the Eucharist, Jesus does all this for us his sheep. The Eucharist is the source of our life. In every Mass, Jesus shares his divine life anew with us. Through the Eucharist he channels to us all the gifts and graces we need for our journeying through life. Above all he makes himself very present to us to assure us of his infinite love. If you ever watched a shepherd tending a small flock of sheep, you probably observed a little lamb approaching the shepherd and nudging him to receive a little pat on the head and then gambol off to the flock. In each eucharistic celebration, Jesus gives us that same loving attention.

As we contemplate the unfathomable goodness of God in the Mass, we can pray:

> Worthy is the Lamb that was slain to receive power and riches, wisdom and strength, honor and glory and praise. (Rv 5:12)

Some additional thoughts for contemplation can be found in:

> Ezekiel 34:1-31 — Separation of the sheep
> Psalm 23 — The Shepherd Psalm

SIXTEEN

ON THE HOLY MOUNTAIN

Luke 9:28-36

JESUS and his prayer-team — Peter, John, and James — "went up onto a mountain to pray." A tremendous transformation took place while they were at prayer. "While he was praying his face changed in appearance and his clothes became dazzling white."

Moses and Elijah, representing the Law and Prophets, "appeared in glory and spoke of his passage, which he was about to fulfill in Jerusalem." Moses and Elijah appeared to confirm that which was about to happen in his suffering and death and which would fulfill the prophecies and replace the Law.

There are many parallels in the Mass.

Jesus invites us to come with him to the mountain, to the altar of Tabor. He invites us, like he did Peter, John, and James, to come aside to pray with him.

In the Liturgy of the Word, the plan of God for our salvation is reconfirmed. Just as Moses and Elijah gave meaning to what was about to happen according to God's plan, so the Word of the Lord in

49

Mass each day gives meaning to all the happenings in our life.

On Mount Tabor, Jesus was transfigured and became resplendent. For a brief moment his divinity broke the shell of his humanity and the apostles witnessed his glory. In the Eucharist, Jesus remains hidden under the appearances of bread and wine. Occasionally he may gift us with an experiential awareness of his presence to bolster our faith, to reassure us of his loving presence.

The faith of Peter, John, and James was strengthened to such an extent that they could partially understand the tragedy of his passion and death which was to occur in the not-too-distant future, and that they might also be a pillar of support to the other apostles.

We have the privilege of meeting Jesus eucharistically each day at Mass. In the Mass we are nourished, strengthened, renewed, so that we can accompany Jesus wherever he may lead us that day.

Listen to the Father say to us at Mass: "This is my Son, my Chosen One. Listen to him."

With Peter, let your heart rejoice: "Master, how good it is for us to be here."

Additional suggestions for prayer:
  2 Peter 1:12-19 — The first Pope gives his
                    testimony
  Matthew 3:13-17 — To listen is to pray

SEVENTEEN

THE EUCHARIST AND THE HOLY SPIRIT

John 7:37-39

WHEN Jesus finished his redemptive work on earth, he handed over the ministry of sanctification to the Holy Spirit. How aptly it is said: "From the pierced side of Christ the Church is born." The visible evidence of the presence and power of the Holy Spirit was manifested on the first public Pentecost with the outpouring of the Spirit and the signs and wonders which followed.

The Holy Spirit continues the sanctification of the Church, especially through the sacrificial and sacramental channels of the Eucharist. In fact the Eucharist is a special intercessory prayer addressed to the Holy Spirit. In speaking of the Holy Spirit, Jesus invites us: "If anyone thirst let him come to me: let him drink who believes in me" (Jn 7:37).

In Eucharistic Prayer II, we plead: "Let your Spirit come upon these gifts to make them holy, so that they may become for us the body and blood of our Lord, Jesus Christ." Yes, we are certain that the bread and wine will become the body and blood of Jesus, but we pray that we will really recognize and appreciate it as the very presence of Jesus. We do accept it in our minds, but we need to accept it with our hearts in order to live the Eucharist.

In Eucharistic Prayer III we confess: "All life, all holiness comes from you through your Son, Jesus Christ our Lord, by the working of the Holy Spirit." This is an expression of faith in the fact that the Holy Spirit is the very source of our sanctification.

Jesus becomes Eucharist for us; we in turn must become Eucharist to others. After being nourished and replenished with the eucharistic presence of Jesus, we must be able to radiate his love and his joy in our daily environment. We need a dynamic, vibrant faith which is a special gift of the Spirit; hence we ask that "by the power of the Holy Spirit" our faith will remain a faith of commitment.

We recognize too that we are unable of ourselves to give adequate praise and glory to God; hence we pray in every Mass:

Through him, with him, in him, in the unity of the Holy Spirit, all glory and honor is yours almighty Father for ever and ever. Amen.

To continue this theme in prayer we suggest:
    Romans 8:26-27 — Teaches us to pray
    Romans 5:1-11 — The Holy Spirit is an inexhaustible source of love

EIGHTEEN

JESUS HEALS AT MASS

Mark 2:1-12

JESUS always healed those who came to him
with confidence and faith. "He healed all who
were in need of healing" (Lk 9:11). He always
healed the whole person as he did when the four
men brought the paralytic to him. Apparently, they
asked only for a healing of his paralysis. Jesus was so
pleased with their faith that he also healed the man
spiritually. "My son, your sins are forgiven."

Jesus invites us to join him at the Eucharist for
many reasons. One reason is the fact that we all
stand in need of healing. Jesus instituted the
Eucharist as a channel of healing. The Mass is a
powerful source of healing.

We begin the eucharistic celebration by pausing
to beg Jesus to heal our sinfulness, our many
weaknesses, our faults and failures, our lack of love
and gratitude. We ask him to remove all barriers
which may prevent him from working freely in us
and through us.

We begin the Mass with the Penitential Rite in
which we humbly turn to our triune God to ask forgiveness and healing: "Lord, have mercy. Christ

have mercy. Lord, have mercy." The celebrant then asks that God may impart his loving mercy to us as he prays, "May almighty God have mercy on us, forgive us our sins, and bring us to everlasting life."

The whole Mass is a prayer for mercy and forgiveness; however, at times we beg more explicitly for God's forgiveness. After we have addressed ourselves to the Father in the words Jesus taught us, we continue with a prayer for healing:

> Deliver us, Lord, from evil, and grant us peace in our day. In your mercy keep us free from sin and protect us from all anxiety as we wait in joyful hope for the coming of our Savior, Jesus Christ.

Just before Holy Communion we are cognizant once again of our unworthiness and we pray with the words of John the Baptist: "Lamb of God, you take away the sins of the world: have mercy on us."

We begin and end the Mass with the assurance of loving forgiveness and healing because Jesus promised, "Whatever you ask in my name, I will do" (Jn 14:13).

To continue your contemplation on this theme the following Scriptures may be helpful:

> Hebrews 9:11-15 — Jesus is our redeemer
> James 5:16 — The acknowledgement of our sinfulness is therapeutic

NINETEEN

THE HEALING POWER OF THE GOOD NEWS AT MASS

Matthew 11:2-6

JESUS wanted to be known as a healer because in this way he could manifest his great love for us. When the disciples of John the Baptist asked Jesus, "Are you 'He who is to come' or do we look for another?" Jesus simply replied by pointing to his healing mission. One aspect of that healing was the power of his Word: "The poor have the good news preached to them."

On another occasion Jesus assured us of the healing power of his Word: "You are clean already, thanks to the word I have spoken to you" (Jn 15:3).

Jesus speaks his Word to us in the Liturgy of the Word at each eucharistic celebration. The Second Vatican Council reminds us that Jesus is present in his Word. "He (Jesus) is present in His Word, since it is He Himself who speaks to us when the holy Scriptures are read in the Church." (Constitution on the Sacred Liturgy, Par. 7).

As Jesus speaks to us in the Liturgy of the Word, we find inspiration, motivation, hope, and comfort which are often healing balm for us. As we listen to his Word, a conversion is taking place within us. As we expose our thinking and attitudes to the Word of Jesus, we may discover that they are not totally in conformity with the mind and heart of Jesus. Almost without our being aware of it, his Word begins to mold and transform us.

Hearing his Word read and explained at Mass helps us keep our focus on God as our prime priority in life. So easily our real objectives and ideals in life can become hazy and clouded as the demands of the secular world encroach more and more upon us. We need his Word as a guideline to help us keep our sights riveted on real values here in our earthly exile.

Also, through his powerful presence in his Word, a transformation is effected within us. St. Paul advises us to put on the new man, to acquire a fresh spiritual way of thinking, to have this mind in you which was in Christ Jesus. His Word united with his eucharistic presence has a tremendous transforming power if we permit it to become operative in our lives. Jesus told us that apart from him we can do nothing; however, the implication is that with him we can do all things.

Some additional thoughts for contemplation can be found in:

> Hebrews 4:12-13 — God's Word is living and effective
> Matthew 13:4-23 — The seed is the Word of God.

TWENTY

EUCHARIST: A HEALING PRESENCE

1 Corinthians 11:17-34

IN our human experience, we know how healing the presence of a friend can be. Perhaps you can recall a time when you were lonely, discouraged, depressed, and a friend surprised you with a visit. You, no doubt, experienced a real healing as his or her sunny, cheery disposition reached out in loving concern to you. If a human presence can have such a therapeutic value, how much more powerful is the healing of the divine presence of Jesus!

Jesus assured us of his abiding presence with us: "Know that I am with you always, until the end of the world" (Mt 28:20). He reminds us that he did not come into the world as a guest, but that he came to stay. "Anyone who loves me will be true to my word, and my Father will love him; we will come to him and make our dwelling place with him" (Jn 14:23).

When Jesus instituted the Holy Eucharist, he gave us the gift of himself and the assurance that he will remain with us. The Eucharist is the tangible sign of his presence and he bade us, "Do this in remembrance of me." Each day is Christmas Day because each day Jesus is born anew on our altars.

Jesus gave us the gift of his eucharistic presence so that he could abide "with" us. A person radiating peace and joy can certainly electrify others by his very presence. Thus Jesus, with all his love, peace, and joy, reaches out in healing to us at all times in the Eucharist.

Even more, Jesus comes to dwell "within" us at each Mass. His indwelling has a powerful transforming effect. He calms our fears, teaches us patience, helps us reach out in love to others. He heals our wounded feelings. He cleanses us of our resentments, self-centeredness, and pride.

Martha reminds us of the healing presence of Jesus: "Lord, if you had been here, my brother would never have died" (Jn 11:21).

This is the Good News. Jesus fulfilled his promise when he said, "I will not leave you orphaned; I will come back to you" (Jn 14:18).

The Lord is saying, "Know that I am with you always until the end of the world." He is continuing to heal you each day.

To continue your prayer with the healing presence of Jesus, read:

> John 1:10-14 — Jesus is not a guest; he is here to stay
>
> Ezekiel 36:25-28 — The prophet foretells the healing power of God with us

TWENTY-ONE

THE EUCHARIST: SOURCE OF PEACE

John 14:27

Peace is a word which is on everyone's lips and a thought which is in the hearts of many. We speak of peace not only as a cessation of military aggression, but primarily as a state of harmony in the hearts of men.

In the Old Testament the Messiah was announced as the "Prince of Peace" (Isaiah 9:5). His birth was proclaimed as the new era of peace "to guide our feet into the way of peace" (Lk 1:79). Jesus himself established his kingdom as a reign of peace. "Peace is my farewell to you, my peace is my gift to you" (Jn 14:27). After his resurrection, his first greeting was, "Peace be with you."

Through the eucharistic celebration, Jesus continued his work of establishing and implementing his peace in our hearts. Peace comes into our hearts only through our personal intimate relationship with Jesus. At Mass this relationship is deepened and enriched.

At Mass the entire Body of Christ comes together to pray for peace. As his family we pray, "Lord, may this sacrifice, which has made our peace with you, advance the peace and salvation of all the world" (Eucharistic Prayer III.) Later we pray for peace as a healing balm: "Deliver us, Lord, from every evil, and grant us peace in our day."

As we become more and more aware of the indwelling of the risen Jesus within us, we are more and more at peace. How appropriately the Church incorporates her prayer for peace just before Holy Communion, when Jesus comes to us to augment our peace by his very presence.

> "Lord Jesus Christ, you said to your apostles: I leave you peace, my peace I give you. Look not on our sins, but on the faith of your Church and grant us the peace and unity of your kingdom where you live forever and ever. Amen"

Then follows the celebrant's greeting, "The peace of the Lord be with you always."

How significant, too, that we pause to extend to one another that great gift and greeting — Peace — and then continue to pray, "Lamb of God, you take away the sins of the world: grant us peace."

The Eucharist is the channel of his peace, the very source and fountain of all peace. Jesus invites us that he may fill us with this peace which the world cannot give.

Contemplate the gift of peace as found in:
Romans 14:12-19 — Fruit of the Spirit
Philippians 4:4-9 — The peace and joy of the
Lord

TWENTY-TWO

THE MASS AND COMMUNITY

Ephesians 4:1-6

THE Holy Spirit is operative in and through the
Mass. He accomplishes his work of purification
and sanctification through the avenues which Jesus
instituted, especially through the eucharistic sacrifice.

The Mass is a powerful prayer of intercession. In
each Mass we implore the Holy Spirit to draw us into genuine Christian community. The Holy Spirit is
the source of unity and the builder of community.
St. Paul admonishes us to "Make every effort to
preserve the unity which has the Spirit as its origin
and peace as its binding force" (Eph 4:3).

The Eucharist also encourages and strengthens
community. Paul reminds us of this truth when he
says, "Is not the bread we break a sharing in the
body of Christ? Because the loaf of bread is one, we,
many though we are, are one body, for we all par-
take of one loaf" (1 Cor 10:16-17).

In fervent prayer to the Holy Spirit at Mass, we
beg, "May all of us who share in the body and blood
of Christ be brought together in unity by the Holy
Spirit" (Eucharistic Prayer II).

Also, we implore the Holy Spirit: "Grant that we, who are nourished by his body and blood, may be filled with his Holy Spirit, and become one body, one spirit in Christ" (Eucharistic Prayer III).

Our prime duty in life is to give praise and glory to God. One way in which we can do this is to work toward forming genuine Christian community, being of one mind and one heart with Jesus our eternal Highpriest; therefore, we pray, "Lord, look upon this sacrifice which you have given to your Church: and by your Holy Spirit, gather all who share this bread and wine into the one body of Christ, a living sacrifice of praise" (Eucharistic Prayer IV).

Notice that in all these prayers we recognize that the Holy Spirit alone can draw us into a real community of love.

We are all baptized into the Trinitarian life. The Trinity, the most perfect community, is bound together by an infinite love; consequently, we are destined for community. Unless we are striving for a community built on love, we shall not achieve genuine happiness in this life.

St. Paul reminds us: "You are the temple of the living God, just as God has said: 'I will dwell with them and walk among them. I will be their God and they shall be my people' " (2 Cor 6:16).

To continue your contemplative prayer with this thought we suggest:

Romans 8:14-27 — The Holy Spirit leads us into
community

Colossians 3:12-17 — How community is
formed

TWENTY-THREE

PEOPLE OF GOD

John 17:21-23

FROM personal experience we know what a source of joy and comfort it is to be surrounded by a loving family. How precious are those close friends who love us like brothers and sisters. Our friends and family are special gifts from God. We are social beings and we need the encouragement and support of those who care about us. We need to be loved.

Jesus knew how badly we would need one another. At the first Eucharist in the Upper Room, he prayed fervently that his followers would be so closely united in love that they would become a closely knit community — his special family, his Body.

Community can be formed only when we are first united with Jesus in love. A community is founded on love and cannot be formed solely on laws and regulations. The highest level of love is union. Jesus pleaded with his Father that such a community could be formed among his followers: "That they may be one as you, Father, are in me, and I in you; I pray that they may be one in us that the world may believe that you sent me. I have given them the glory you gave me that they may be one as we are one—I living in them, you living in me—that their unity may be complete" (Jn 17:21-23).

The Holy Eucharist is a means of strengthening and building community. Just as Jesus prayed, we, too, pray at each eucharistic celebration for this unity in a loving community. In Eucharistic Prayer II together with the whole Church we pray:

> May all of us who share in the body and blood of Christ be brought together in unity by the Holy Spirit.

The Holy Spirit is the source of love. He is the builder of community, the source of unity; hence we implore his aid in Eucharistic Prayer III: "Grant that we, who are nourished by his body and blood, may be filled with his Holy Spirit and become one body, one spirit in Christ."

In Eucharistic Prayer IV we beg the Holy Spirit to form us into a family of love:

> Lord, look upon this sacrifice which you have given to your Church; and by your Holy Spirit, gather all who share this bread and wine into the one body of Christ a living sacrifice of praise.

Be assured that the prayer of Jesus and ours will be answered if we are receptive to the divine operations of the Holy Spirit within us.

To continue your contemplation we suggest:
1 Corinthians 12:12-26—Our body has many members
Ephesians 4:1-6—Peace is the matrix

TWENTY-FOUR

THE OUR FATHER IS EUCHARIST

Luke 11:1-2

"**O**NE day he was praying in a certain place. When he had finished one of his disciples asked him: 'Lord, teach us to pray' . . ." (Lk 11:1). It was then that Jesus taught them the Our Father. It is unlikely that Jesus gave them the exact formula of this prayer. He probably told them that this should be the attitude on which their prayer should be based.

The "Our Father" belongs in the Mass. In fact it is a kind of Eucharist itself. As we pray the Lord's Prayer, we are fulfilling our primary duties toward our loving Father. We can best fulfill these duties with and through Jesus at Mass.

In this prayer we call God *our Father*. As we offer the Eucharist, we are acknowledging God as our loving Father and showing our complete dependence upon him.

We pray that *his name may be hallowed*. The most perfect way we have to give honor and glory to his name is through Jesus. The whole theme of the Mass is to unite our praise and thanksgiving to the Father with the praise of Jesus. This means that the

Father is the center and focus of our lives. Our own name is not to be highlighted. We recognize who we are and who God is.

"*Your kingdom come*" means giving up our rebellious wills. From the moment we say "Our Father," we give ourselves totally to his plans for our life. We need to renew this commitment at each Mass.

Scripture tells us: "It is a fearful thing to fall into the hands of the living God" (Heb 10:31). He is a living God who loves us. Jesus loves us so much he gave his life for us. At each Mass we join him to give our lives to God who loves us. Love knows no limits.

God is gift. He pours himself out in our lives. Creation, the Incarnation, the Redemption are efforts God used to make himself immanent in our lives.

At Mass, Jesus gives our lives back to the Father along with his own. In Communion, Jesus gives us the life of the Father with his own. "On that day you will know that I am in my Father, and you in me, and I in you" (Jn 14:20).

The more we receive the more we have to give back. And the more we give back, the more shall be given to us and the more we shall have to continue to give back. The greatest mistake that we can make is to keep our lives to ourselves.

To continue your contemplative prayer, read:
    Romans 8:14-17 — God's family
    Matthew 6:25-34 — Our primary objective

TWENTY-FIVE

OUR PRAYER TO THE FATHER

Luke 11:3-4

ONE day I noticed a billboard with only four short words on it. There was no name of a sponsor nor any legend, since it was self-explanatory. It read: GIVE US THIS DAY. What a perfect prayer begging God for all we need. What a proper attitude for prayer recognizing our poverty and total dependence upon our caring Father.

How appropriately these thoughts fit into the Eucharist, since the Mass is a prayer of petition and a recognition that by ourselves we can accomplish nothing. In the Mass, Jesus takes our needs as his own and presents them to the Father in our name.

Jesus taught us to present our petitions to the Father in this manner in the prayer he gave us. The Church has rightly made the Lord's Prayer an integral part of the Mass.

"Give us each day our daily bread" is a humble acknowledgment that we must depend totally on our loving Abba's providential care. In the Mass, we present our needs to the Father through the powerful mediation of Jesus, who reminds us that

"Apart from me you can do nothing" (Jn 15:5).

"Forgive our sins" is a plea for mercy and compassion which arises from the recognition that we are all sinners in God's sight and God alone can forgive us. We need his redemptive love every day of our lives. Each day at Mass we beg again for his forgiveness.

When we have experienced the peace his forgiveness brings us, then we can more easily forgive others. In the Eucharist, we are taken up to Calvary where we can hear all the insults, mockery, blasphemies hurled at Jesus; then we hear his voice rising loud and clear above the din of the derision: "Father, forgive them; they do not know what they are doing." (Lk 23:34). After such a prayer experience, we can more easily say; "For we too forgive all who do us wrong."

"Subject us not to the trial" is a plea recognizing the weakness of our sinful nature and our own inability to counteract every temptation in our lives. Jesus assures us as he promised St. Paul: "My grace is enough for you, for in weakness power reaches perfection" (2 Cor 12:9).

As we contemplate this bounteous goodness of God, we joyously proclaim, "For the kingdom, the power and the glory are yours, now and forever."

Continue to contemplate God's providential, healing, forgiving love:

Jeremiah 29:11-14 — God has plans for us for every moment of the day

Psalm 32 — The Lord absolves

TWENTY-SIX

ON THE ROAD TO EMMAUS

Luke 24:13-26

I N spite of all the technological advances in artificial lighting, we are still not able to duplicate the natural light of God's sun. For example, a piece of cloth under artificial light will have various shades, shadows, and tints which are dispelled when we take it into the natural light. X-rays help us penetrate beyond what our natural vision can see, but even this achievement is minimized when we ponder God's creative lights in the sun, moon, and stars.

We can draw an analogy for our own lives from this fact. At the beginning of Mass we come closer to the Risen Jesus. As we do so, we can see our faults and failures, our weaknesses and sinfulness more clearly and objectively. As we come into the sunshine of the presence of Jesus, our faults are more apparent and our rationalizations become more transparent. This is why the Church leads us into the Penitential Rite in the Mass that we might see ourselves as we are and turn to the Lord to ask his healing and forgiveness. This is an ideal way to prepare us to meet Jesus as he comes to us in Word and Sacrament. He can heal us of anything which would obstruct his working freely in us and through us.

This is precisely what took place on the road to Emmaus. Presumably the two disciples were on their way home after the tragic events of the past few days. They had followed Jesus with great expectancy. "We were hoping that he was the one who would set Israel free" (Lk 24:21).

Now their hopes were shattered. Their dream-castles tumbled into ruins. They were disappointed, disheartened, discouraged, and depressed. It was then that Jesus had to jar them out of the channel of their self-centered thinking. "What little sense you have! How slow you are to believe all that the prophets have announced! Did not the Messiah have to undergo all this so as to enter into his glory!" (Lk 24:25-26).

Each day as we prayerfully prepare to celebrate the Eucharist, Jesus wants us to see the barriers and roadblocks we set up in our own lives. How gently he leads us to recognize them. He may even permit a little tension, but always with peace. Then as we begin Mass, we pause that we might present them to him once again for healing and forgiveness.

Suggestions for continued prayer:
Luke 7:36-50 — The sinful woman
Matthew 5:23-24 — Reconciliation precedes
oblation

TWENTY-SEVEN

THE LITURGY OF THE WORD

Luke 24:27,32

WHEN we receive a personal letter from some-
one very near and dear to us, we may react in
either of the following two ways. First, we may
read between the lines. If we know the person well,
we can read with greater empathy because we understand the circumstances and the conditions
about which he or she is writing. Secondly, we do
not actually read the letter. Our eyes may follow
the written words, but we really hear the person
speaking to us. Each person has his or her distinc-
tive voice with its peculiar quality, timbre, and
tonality.

As we get to know Jesus more personally each
day, as we begin to know him more with our heart
rather than with our head, then his Word becomes
a personal message to us. As he speaks to us, we
begin to capture his mentality, his attitudes, his
heart.

The Fathers of Vatican II told us: "He (Jesus) is
present in His word, since it is He Himself who
speaks when the holy scriptures are read in the
Church" (Constitution on the Sacred Liturgy, Par. 7).

This is what occurred on the road to Emmaus. We find the formula for the eucharistic celebration taking place here. Jesus chided the disciples for their lack of faith: "What little sense you have!" This is the Penitential Rite. Then he went into the Liturgy of the Word immediately: "Beginning, then, with Moses and all the prophets he interpreted for them every passage of Scripture which referred to him" (Lk 24:27).

How attentively the disciples listened to that Word. What power was in his Word! They had to admit, "were not our hearts burning inside us as he talked to us on the road and explained the Scriptures to us?" (Lk 24:32).

Each day Jesus speaks to us through his Word, especially at Mass and in our contemplative prayer. His Word has the power to inspire and motivate us for each day's duties. His Word effects a conversation within us as we expose our thoughts and feelings to his Word. As we ponder his Word, a transformation takes place within us. We are acquiring a spiritual way of thinking. We are putting on the new man. We have the mind of Jesus in us. Our attitudes are becoming those of Jesus.

Thank him for his Word. Thank him for the power of his Word.

Suggested passages to continue prayer with this theme:

2 Timothy 3:16 — Scripture is the source of wisdom

John 15:9-17 — Joy is God's gift to us

TWENTY-EIGHT

EUCHARIST IN EMMAUS

Luke 24:28-31

WERE you ever embarrassed when an unexpec-
ted visitor dropped in and caught you un-
prepared to receive him. Perhaps on some occasion
you were expecting a certain number of guests for
dinner and without warning an extra person or two
just came along.

Jesus understands this predicament; hence, he
never forces himself on us. He respects our free will.
He waits for an invitation.

When he and the two disciples arrived at the
village of Emmaus. . ."he acted as if he were going
farther." It was only when they pressed him to
"Stay with us," that "he went in to stay with them."

Jesus invites us daily to come to his eucharistic
banquet. He does not force himself upon us. He pa-
tiently waits for our acceptance of his invitation.
How eagerly he awaits our RSVP!

When we accept his invitation to unite ourselves
with him in the eucharistic celebration, only then
does he reveal himself to us in various ways:

1. He comes that he may nourish and strengthen
us for all the exigencies of that day.

2. He comes that he may reveal himself to us in a deeper, richer way. Perhaps we have momentarily forgotten about his loving us just as we are. His eucharistic presence guarantees and assures us of his abiding presence with us and his loving us just as we are.

3. He reveals himself to us to give us the assurance that of ourselves we can do nothing, but with him we can do all things.

4. He comes that he may unite himself with our praise and thanksgiving, thus enabling us to fulfill our prime duty of worshiping and praising our loving Father in heaven.

5. He comes that he may remain with us; also, that we may be one with him.

Continue to listen to Jesus at the core of your being as he speaks to you in:

> Matthew 11:28-30 — A personal invitation from Jesus
>
> John 6:25-71 — Jesus is the source of everything we need

TWENTY-NINE

A CALL TO DISCIPLESHIP

Luke 24:33-35

JESUS calls all of us into discipleship. A disciple is a person who follows the master, not only to receive the information he imparts, not only to learn his techniques, but also to strive to capture his mentality and attitudes, even his personality.

Jesus calls us into discipleship; then, he conditions us in various ways. Only after we have made our commitment does he send us forth.

The disciples on the road to Emmaus were already followers of Jesus, but they were about to give up because they were discouraged.

1. When Jesus met them he began to recondition them as he drew their attention to the fact that their faith was weak since it centered too much on self. He began to prepare them for a deeper commitment by explaining the scriptures to them. "Beginning, then, with Moses and all the prophets, he interpreted for them every passage of Scripture which referred to him" (Lk 24:27).

2. He further prepared them for their ministry by sharing his divine life with them when "he took bread, pronounced the blessing, then, broke the

bread and begin to distribute it to them" (Lk 24:30).

3. Finally they were commissioned to bring the Good News to their community and to the world. "They got up immediately and returned to Jerusalem" (Lk 24:33).

This is the import of the Mass for us. Jesus invites us each day to join him in the Eucharist. He has called us into discipleship. In the Eucharist he continues to condition us and prepare us for our ministry.

Jesus comes to share his divine life with us. We can say with Paul, "The life I live now is not my own; Christ is living in me" (Gal 2:20). Jesus implants his divine life in us so that we can radiate his love, joy, and peace to others. This is our mission in life.

Jesus has become Eucharist for us; now he asks us to become Eucharist to everyone who crosses our path. He reminds us of "How beautiful upon the mountains are the feet of him who brings glad tidings" (Is 52:7). This is the import of the dismissal at Mass. It is not merely an announcement that Mass is over; but rather it is a commission to become Eucharist to others. "Go in peace to *love* and *serve* the Lord."

This is our mission in life. Each day in the Eucharist we are better equipped to carry out this apostolate.

Matthew 28:18-20 — Commissioned by Jesus
Acts 1:1-8 — Empowered to bring the Good
News

THIRTY

THE MASS: A PERFECT PREPARATION FOR DEATH

Romans 6:3-11

THE eucharistic celebration is a comforting, consoling, and peaceful preparation for death. In the Mass we commemorate the passion, death, and resurrection of Jesus. We do not merely recall the paschal mystery; but we actually relive it with the risen Jesus.

In the Eucharist we re-enact the gift of Jesus to the Father. We hear Jesus say, "The Father loves me for this: that I lay down my life to take it up again. No one takes it from me: I lay it down freely" (Jn 10:17-18).

Jesus loves the Father with an infinite love. He assured us that he loves us with that same love because he says, "As the Father has loved me, so I have loved you" (Jn 15:9). Jesus' gift is a complete kenosis. He gave his last drop of blood as an outpouring of this total love.

After he had given his very life, he "had the power to take it up again." (Jn 10:18). He rose from the dead to give us assurance that he wanted to share his risen life with us. He initiated us into his risen life at the moment of our Baptism. He implements that divine life in us at each eucharistic celebration.

The eucharistic celebration is an ideal preparation for our death. In the Mass we offer ourselves, in fact our very lives, to our loving Father. Our gift is transformed through the Consecration when Jesus unites our gift to his own gift of himself. It becomes an acceptable gift and the Father is pleased with our gift. Just as in the Eucharist Jesus shared his risen life, so in death he shares more completely his divine life with us. Death is a doorway through which we enter into a total union of love with the Holy Trinity. We are incorporated more completely into that perfect community of love.

Each day at Mass we prepare for our death by offering our lives as Paul reminds us: "Every time, then, you eat this bread and drink this cup, you proclaim the death of the Lord until he comes" (1 Cor 11:26). Each day we are reminded of the transforming power of the Mass as Jesus transforms our lives by filling us with his own divine life. In death our life is restored to us in a more perfect way. We share more totally in the divine life of Jesus.

We can fearlessly give our lives because we are offering them "through him, with him, and in him. . . ." And we hear Jesus say, "No one who comes to me will I reject. . . . Him I will raise up on the last day" (Jn 6:37,40).

Pray often with the thoughts found in:
1 Corinthians 15:44-58 — Resurrection victory
over death
John 17:24-26 — Jesus prays for all believers

THIRTY-ONE

THE MASS: OUR WEDDING BANQUET

Revelation 19:5-10

Our whole Christian living revolves around the Mass — the central act of worship of the Father, Son and Holy Spirit. It is the "summit toward which the activity of the Church is directed" (The Constitution on the Liturgy, Par. 10).

In the Eucharist, we celebrate the victory of Jesus as we relive the whole paschal mystery of his suffering, death, and resurrection. Mystically we relive it until the day when we will finally and permanently offer ourselves with Jesus to the Father at the moment of our death. St. Paul reminds us: "Every time, then, you eat this bread and drink this cup, you proclaim the death of the Lord until he comes" (1 Cor 11:26).

The Second Vatican Council calls the Mass "the memorial of his death and resurrection: a sacrament of love, a sign of unity, a bond of charity, a paschal banquet in which Christ is eaten, the mind is filled with grace and a pledge of future glory is given us" (The Constitution on the Liturgy, Par. 47).

The eucharistic celebration is the victory song of

Jesus. It is also our song of victory. It is our invitation to become the bride of the Lamb. The theme of marriage uniting God with his people is used frequently in Scripture — already in the Old Testament. It is a biblical metaphor used to describe the covenant relationship between God and his people. "As a bridegroom rejoices in his bride so shall your God rejoice in you" (Is 62:5).

In the New Testament this metaphor is used to express the vital union between Christ and his Church. St. Paul says, "I have given you in marriage to one husband, presenting you as a chaste virgin to Christ." (2 Cor 11:2). This symbol is used to describe the intimate and indissoluble union between us and Jesus. We relive this truth in each eucharistic celebration.

Each Mass takes us to the threshold of heaven, into the vestibule of our eternal union with the Father, Son and Holy Spirit. Each eucharistic celebration deepens our relationship with Jesus and prepares us more fully for the final wedding banquet.

What a tremendous privilege is ours! How realistically we can rejoice in the beatitude: "Happy are they who have been invited to the wedding feast of the Lamb" (Rev 19:9).

If you wish to pray further with this theme we suggest:

      Hosea 2:16-25 — In the desert we find God.
      Ephesians 5:25-27 — Jesus prepares the
                             Church